Copyright © 2023 by Chester Madison (Author)

We hope this book has been informative and helpful on your journey to understanding and celebrating older adults. Thank you for your interest and support!

"The most important thing is to win, not just to play good football."
Pep Guardiola, Manchester City Manager

"If you want to be a champion, you have to score more goals than the opponent."
Jose Mourinho, AS Roma Manager

"It's not just about winning, it's about winning with style."
Arsène Wenger, Former Arsenal Manager

"The difference between a successful person and others is not a lack of strength, not a lack of knowledge, but rather a lack of will."
Vince Lombardi, Former American Football Coach (this quote is often used in football as well)

"In football, the result is an impostor. You can do things really, really well but not win. There's something greater than the result, more lasting - a legacy."
Xavi, Former Barcelona Midfielder

"The ball is the most important thing. It's the only thing that never gets tired."

Jürgen Klopp, Liverpool Manager

"I don't believe skill was, or ever will be, the result of coaches. It is a result of a love affair between the child and the ball."
Roy Keane, Former Manchester United Midfielder

"Football is not just about winning, it's about playing with passion and giving your best every time you step onto the pitch."
Diego Simeone, Atlético Madrid Manager

Table of Contents

Introduction 7

Overview of the book and its purpose 7

The significance of Rehhagel, Capello, and Eriksson in the world of football 9

Brief background information about each person 12

How their coaching philosophies differ from each other 15

Chapter 1: Otto Rehhagel 18

Early life and career as a player 18

Transition to coaching 21

Success with Werder Bremen and Kaiserslautern 24

Leading Greece to their first-ever major tournament victory at Euro 2004 26

Coaching achievements after Euro 2004 28

Rehhagel's coaching style and tactics 30

Chapter 2: Fabio Capello 32

Early life and playing career 32

Transition to coaching 34

Success with AC Milan and Real Madrid 36

International management experiences 38

Leading England to qualify for the 2010 World Cup 40

Coaching style and tactics 43

Chapter 3: Sven-Göran Eriksson 45

Early life and playing career 45

Transition to coaching..49

Success with IFK Göteborg, Benfica, and Lazio 51

England national team experiences and controversies .. 53

Coaching achievements after leaving England 55

Eriksson's coaching style and tactics 57

Conclusion **60**

A summary of each coach's impact on football 60

How their coaching philosophies have influenced the game 63

The legacy of Rehhagel, Capello, and Eriksson 66

Final thoughts and recommendations for further reading 69

Key Terms and Definitions 73

Supporting Materials 75

Introduction

Overview of the book and its purpose

Football, also known as soccer in some parts of the world, is one of the most popular and beloved sports worldwide. From the streets of Brazil to the stadiums of Europe and Asia, football has the power to bring people together, to inspire and to entertain. At the heart of this beautiful game are the coaches and managers who lead their teams to glory, who shape the tactics and the culture of the sport, and who leave a lasting legacy for future generations.

In this book, we will explore the lives and careers of three exceptional football coaches who have left an indelible mark on the game. These coaches are Otto Rehhagel, Fabio Capello, and Sven-Göran Eriksson. What sets them apart is not only their success and longevity in the sport but also their age. Each of these coaches has worked in football beyond the age of 75, defying the conventional wisdom that coaching is a young person's game. By doing so, they have demonstrated the power of experience, expertise, and resilience in the face of challenges and change.

Our purpose in this book is to examine the winning formulas of football as embodied by these three coaches. We will delve into their backgrounds, their achievements, their coaching styles, and their legacies. By doing so, we hope to offer insights and inspiration to football enthusiasts, coaches, players, and anyone who wants to learn from the best.

In the following chapters, we will cover each coach in turn, starting with Otto Rehhagel, the German coach who led Greece to their improbable victory in Euro 2004. We will then move on to Fabio Capello, the Italian coach who won multiple titles with AC Milan and Real Madrid, and who guided England to the World Cup in 2010. Finally, we will explore the career of Sven-Göran Eriksson, the Swedish coach who enjoyed success with IFK Göteborg, Benfica, and Lazio, and who faced both praise and criticism during his tenure as England's national team coach.

Throughout the book, we will examine each coach's approach to coaching, their tactical innovations, their leadership style, and their impact on the sport. We will also explore how their experiences and philosophies can inform and inspire the next generation of football coaches and players.

We hope that this book will offer a fresh perspective on football coaching, celebrating the achievements of three remarkable coaches and offering insights and inspiration for anyone who loves the game.

The significance of Rehhagel, Capello, and Eriksson in the world of football

Football is a sport that has captivated the world for generations, producing countless stars, moments of drama, and memorable matches. Yet, at the heart of this sport are the coaches who lead and inspire their teams, who create winning strategies, and who shape the culture of the game. In this book, we will focus on three exceptional coaches who have left an indelible mark on football: Otto Rehhagel, Fabio Capello, and Sven-Göran Eriksson.

Otto Rehhagel

Otto Rehhagel is a legendary German coach who began his career as a player before transitioning to coaching. He is perhaps best known for his success in leading Greece to their first-ever major tournament victory at Euro 2004, which many consider to be one of the greatest upsets in football history. Rehhagel's tactical innovations and disciplined approach to coaching were critical factors in Greece's triumph, as he molded a group of underdogs into a cohesive and determined team.

Prior to his success with Greece, Rehhagel had already enjoyed a distinguished career in German football. He won the Bundesliga title with Werder Bremen in 1988, and later led Kaiserslautern to the championship in 1998. His ability to build strong and organized defenses, as well as his tactical flexibility and attention to detail, made him one of the most respected coaches in the game.

Fabio Capello

Fabio Capello is an Italian coach who achieved remarkable success both domestically and internationally. He won numerous titles with AC Milan and Real Madrid, two of the most storied clubs in football history. His tactical acumen and ability to motivate players were essential in guiding these clubs to glory. Capello was also known for his discipline and high standards, demanding nothing but the best from his players.

Capello also had success as a national team coach, leading England to qualify for the 2010 World Cup. His ability to adapt to different playing styles and to foster a winning mentality were critical factors in England's qualification campaign. However, Capello was not without controversy during his time as England's coach, particularly over his handling of the captaincy and his perceived rigidity in tactics.

Sven-Göran Eriksson

Sven-Göran Eriksson is a Swedish coach who began his career as a player before transitioning to coaching. He enjoyed success with IFK Göteborg, Benfica, and Lazio, winning numerous titles and earning a reputation as a master tactician. Eriksson's ability to create attacking-minded teams, as well as his ability to adapt to different playing styles, made him a sought-after coach.

Eriksson is perhaps best known for his tenure as the coach of the England national team. He guided England to three consecutive quarter-final appearances at major tournaments, and helped to usher in a new era of attacking football. However, his time as England's coach was not without controversy, particularly over his perceived lack of tactical flexibility and his off-field dalliances.

In summary, Rehhagel, Capello, and Eriksson are three coaches who have achieved remarkable success in the world of football. Their tactical innovations, leadership styles, and ability to motivate players have made them among the most respected coaches in the game. In the following chapters, we will delve deeper into each coach's life and career, examining their coaching philosophies and their impact on the sport.

Brief background information about each person

In this section, we will provide a brief background on each of the three football coaches who are the focus of this book: Otto Rehhagel, Fabio Capello, and Sven-Göran Eriksson.

Otto Rehhagel

Otto Rehhagel is a German football coach who was born on August 9, 1938, in Essen, Germany. He began his playing career as a defender for Rot-Weiss Essen before moving to Hertha Berlin and then Kaiserslautern. Rehhagel retired as a player in 1972 and began his coaching career at Kaiserslautern in 1974.

Rehhagel achieved great success with Kaiserslautern, leading them to the Bundesliga title in 1991. He also won the DFB-Pokal with the club in 1990. In 1995, Rehhagel moved to Werder Bremen, where he won the Bundesliga title in 2004 and the DFB-Pokal in 1999.

Rehhagel is perhaps best known for his work with the Greek national team. He took over as head coach in 2001 and led the team to their first-ever major tournament victory at Euro 2004, where they defeated Portugal in the final. Rehhagel's defensive tactics and disciplined style of play were key to Greece's success.

Fabio Capello

Fabio Capello is an Italian football coach who was born on June 18, 1946, in San Canzian d'Isonzo, Italy. He began his playing career as a midfielder for SPAL and Roma before moving to Juventus in 1970. Capello won four Serie A titles and a European Cup with Juventus before retiring as a player in 1980.

Capello began his coaching career at AC Milan in 1991, where he won four Serie A titles and the Champions League in 1994. He went on to coach Roma, Juventus, Real Madrid, and the England national team. Capello won the Serie A title with Roma in 2001 and with Juventus in 2005 and 2006. He also won La Liga twice with Real Madrid in 1997 and 2007.

Sven-Göran Eriksson

Sven-Göran Eriksson is a Swedish football coach who was born on February 5, 1948, in Torsby, Sweden. He began his playing career as a midfielder for Torsby IF and then moved to IFK Göteborg, where he won the Swedish league title in 1971 and 1982.

Eriksson began his coaching career at Degerfors IF in 1977 before moving to IFK Göteborg in 1979. He won the Swedish league title with IFK Göteborg in 1982 and the UEFA Cup in 1982 and 1987. Eriksson then moved to Benfica in 1989, where he won the Portuguese league title in 1991 and 1994.

Eriksson's most high-profile coaching role was as the manager of the England national team from 2001 to 2006. During his time as England manager, Eriksson led the team to three major tournaments and reached the quarter-finals of the World Cup in 2002 and 2006. Eriksson's coaching style has been described as pragmatic and focused on getting results.

Each of the three football coaches featured in this book has had a long and successful career in the sport, with a coaching philosophy that is unique to their individual style. In this section, we will explore the differences in the coaching philosophies of Otto Rehhagel, Fabio Capello, and Sven-Göran Eriksson.

Otto Rehhagel's coaching philosophy is based on a strong focus on defensive tactics and discipline. His teams are known for their ability to defend well and take advantage of opportunities on the counter-attack. He emphasizes the importance of teamwork, with every player knowing their role and working together towards a common goal. Rehhagel is also known for his meticulous preparation, analyzing the strengths and weaknesses of his opponents to come up with a game plan that maximizes his team's chances of success.

Fabio Capello's coaching philosophy is centered around a strong work ethic and tactical flexibility. His teams are known for their defensive solidity, but also for their ability to attack quickly and effectively. Capello stresses the importance of players understanding their roles within the team, and being willing to adapt to different tactics depending on the opposition. He is a coach who demands discipline and professionalism from his players, and expects them to work hard both on and off the pitch.

Sven-Göran Eriksson's coaching philosophy is based on an attacking style of play, with a focus on possession and creative flair. His teams are known for their technical ability and skillful play, and Eriksson encourages his players to express themselves on the pitch. He also emphasizes the importance of building strong relationships with his players, and creating a positive team spirit that can help drive success on the field. Eriksson is also known for his ability to handle pressure, with a calm and composed demeanor even in high-pressure situations.

While there are certainly differences in the coaching philosophies of Rehhagel, Capello, and Eriksson, there are also similarities. All three coaches have a strong emphasis on discipline and professionalism, and they all prioritize tactical preparation and analysis. They also share a common goal of winning, and have all had considerable success in their coaching careers.

It is these differences and similarities that make the stories of these three coaches so fascinating, and it is our hope that by exploring their individual coaching philosophies in more detail, readers will gain a greater understanding of what it takes to be successful at the highest level of football coaching.

Chapter 1: Otto Rehhagel
Early life and career as a player

Otto Rehhagel, one of the three football coaches featured in this book, has had a long and successful career in the sport. Before becoming a coach, Rehhagel was also a successful player, and his early life and career as a player played a significant role in shaping his coaching philosophy.

Rehhagel was born in Essen, Germany in 1938, and began playing football at a young age. He started his professional career as a defender for Rot-Weiss Essen in 1959, and went on to play for a number of other clubs throughout his playing career, including Hertha BSC Berlin, Kaiserslautern, and Borussia Dortmund.

As a player, Rehhagel was known for his tough-tackling style and his ability to read the game. He was a tenacious defender, and his ability to anticipate the movements of opposing attackers made him a valuable asset to any team he played for. Despite not being the most technically gifted player, Rehhagel's work rate and determination on the pitch earned him a reputation as a reliable and hard-working defender.

One of the defining moments of Rehhagel's playing career came in 1966, when he helped Kaiserslautern win the German Cup. The victory was the first major trophy of

Rehhagel's career, and it helped establish him as one of the top defenders in Germany at the time.

However, it was as a coach that Rehhagel truly made his mark on the world of football. He began his coaching career in the early 1970s, and quickly developed a reputation as a tactical genius. His attention to detail and ability to analyze his opponents' weaknesses set him apart from many of his contemporaries, and he quickly established himself as one of the top coaches in Germany.

Rehhagel's early coaching success came with Werder Bremen, whom he led to the Bundesliga title in 1988. He also had success with Kaiserslautern, whom he guided to the second division title in 1996. However, it was his achievements with the Greek national team that truly cemented his legacy in the world of football.

In 2001, Rehhagel was appointed as the head coach of the Greek national team, a position he held for six years. It was during this time that he led Greece to their first-ever major tournament victory at Euro 2004, a remarkable achievement that stunned the football world. Greece's success at Euro 2004 was largely due to Rehhagel's tactical masterclass, as he organized his team to defend resolutely and take advantage of their opportunities on the counter-attack.

In conclusion, Otto Rehhagel's early life and career as a player played a significant role in shaping his coaching philosophy. As a player, he was known for his tough-tackling style and his ability to read the game, qualities that would later translate into his coaching style. His attention to detail and ability to analyze his opponents' weaknesses set him apart from many of his contemporaries, and he would go on to achieve great success as a coach, particularly with the Greek national team at Euro 2004.

Otto Rehhagel's transition from a football player to a coach was not an easy one. After ending his playing career at the age of 32, he struggled to find a job as a coach. However, his persistence paid off, and he eventually landed his first coaching job at third-tier club Kickers Offenbach in 1974.

Rehhagel quickly made a name for himself as a coach who could get the best out of his players. He led Kickers Offenbach to promotion to the second division in his first season in charge, and the following year he guided them to a fourth-place finish.

In 1977, Rehhagel was appointed as the head coach of Bundesliga club Hertha BSC. He spent two seasons with the club, but was unable to achieve much success due to financial difficulties and a lack of quality players.

Rehhagel's fortunes changed in 1979, when he was appointed as the head coach of Werder Bremen. He quickly transformed the club into one of the top teams in the Bundesliga, leading them to the league title in 1988 and the DFB-Pokal (German Cup) in 1991.

During his time at Werder Bremen, Rehhagel developed a reputation as a tactical mastermind. He was known for his ability to devise game plans that could neutralize the opposition's strengths while exploiting their weaknesses. He also had a keen eye for talent and was instrumental in the development of players such as Miroslav Klose, who went on to become one of Germany's greatest ever strikers.

Rehhagel's success at Werder Bremen led to him being appointed as the head coach of the Greek national team in 2001. He faced a daunting task, as Greece had never qualified for a major tournament and were not considered to be among the strongest teams in Europe.

However, Rehhagel's tactical acumen and motivational skills proved to be a perfect fit for the Greek team. He led them to an unexpected victory at the 2004 European Championships, beating some of the biggest names in European football along the way. It was a remarkable achievement, and Rehhagel became a national hero in Greece.

Rehhagel's success with Greece also earned him a place in football history. He became the oldest coach ever to win a major international tournament, at the age of 65.

Overall, Rehhagel's transition from a player to a coach was marked by hard work, persistence, and a dedication to the game. He faced many challenges along the way, but he never gave up and always believed in his abilities. His success as a coach can be attributed to his tactical brilliance, his ability to motivate players, and his keen eye for talent.

Otto Rehhagel's success as a football coach can be traced back to his time with Werder Bremen and Kaiserslautern in the German Bundesliga.

In 1981, Rehhagel was appointed as the head coach of Werder Bremen. At the time, the club was struggling in the bottom half of the table and was facing relegation. Rehhagel's arrival sparked a remarkable turnaround, as he led the team to a 14th place finish in his first season in charge. The following season, Werder Bremen finished in 4th place, securing qualification for the UEFA Cup. In the 1983/84 season, Rehhagel guided Werder Bremen to their first-ever Bundesliga title. They also reached the final of the DFB-Pokal, but lost to Bayern Munich.

Rehhagel's success with Werder Bremen continued in the following years. He led the team to a second-place finish in the Bundesliga in the 1984/85 season, as well as another DFB-Pokal final appearance in 1989. In total, Rehhagel spent 14 seasons with Werder Bremen, and during that time he transformed the club into one of the most successful teams in Germany.

After leaving Werder Bremen in 1995, Rehhagel took charge of Kaiserslautern, who had just been promoted to the Bundesliga. He led the team to an astonishing Bundesliga title in his first season in charge, making Kaiserslautern the first newly promoted team to win the league in German football history. Rehhagel's tactical acumen was a key factor in Kaiserslautern's success, as he implemented a counter-attacking style that caught many teams off guard. Kaiserslautern's title-winning campaign is still regarded as one of the greatest achievements in Bundesliga history.

Rehhagel's success with Werder Bremen and Kaiserslautern cemented his status as one of the most respected coaches in Germany. His ability to transform struggling teams into title contenders was remarkable, and he was widely praised for his tactical intelligence and attention to detail. Rehhagel's success with these clubs laid the foundation for his later achievements on the international stage with Greece.

Otto Rehhagel's most significant achievement as a football coach was leading Greece to their first-ever major tournament victory at Euro 2004. The Greek national team's victory was a massive surprise, and Rehhagel's tactical masterstrokes and team management were instrumental in achieving this success.

Greece was not considered among the favorites to win the tournament, with many pundits predicting early exits for the team. However, Rehhagel's tactics, based on a solid defense and counter-attacking style, proved to be highly effective in neutralizing more fancied opponents.

In the opening game of the tournament, Greece faced hosts Portugal, who were expected to win comfortably. However, Rehhagel's men produced an outstanding performance, defending resolutely and scoring a late winner through Angelos Basinas to secure a 1-0 victory.

Greece continued to defy the odds, beating defending champions France 1-0 in the quarter-finals and the Czech Republic by the same scoreline in the semi-finals. In the final, Greece faced Portugal again, and once again, Rehhagel's tactics proved to be the difference. Greece scored twice in the first half through Angelos Basinas and

Theodoros Zagorakis, and despite a late goal from Portugal's Cristiano Ronaldo, held on to win 2-1 and lift the trophy.

Rehhagel's achievement with Greece was not just about tactics, however. He also managed to create a strong team spirit and a sense of togetherness within the squad, which was evident in the way the players celebrated their victories together. Rehhagel's leadership qualities were crucial in getting the team to believe in themselves and their ability to achieve something historic.

The victory at Euro 2004 was a remarkable achievement for Rehhagel, who had previously achieved success at club level in Germany but had never won a major international tournament. It was also a significant moment for Greek football, which had never achieved anything comparable before.

In conclusion, Otto Rehhagel's success with Greece at Euro 2004 was one of the greatest achievements in football history. It was a triumph of tactical acumen, team management, and leadership, and it demonstrated the importance of teamwork and belief in achieving success. Rehhagel's legacy in Greek football is secure, and his contribution to the game will be remembered for generations to come.

After leading Greece to their historic Euro 2004 victory, Otto Rehhagel's coaching career continued to flourish, and he achieved more notable successes.

Following the Euro 2004 win, Rehhagel continued to manage the Greek national team until the 2010 World Cup. During this period, Greece qualified for the 2008 European Championship and reached the quarter-finals, where they were knocked out by Germany, the eventual finalists.

Rehhagel's success with Greece caught the attention of German clubs, and in 2007, he returned to the Bundesliga to coach Hertha Berlin. However, his stint with the club was short-lived, and he resigned in February 2008 after only six months in charge.

In 2009, Rehhagel was appointed coach of the Greek club, Kavala FC, where he stayed until 2010. His time with Kavala was not as successful as his tenure with the national team, and the team narrowly avoided relegation from the Greek Super League.

Despite the mixed success with Kavala, Rehhagel remained in demand, and in July 2010, he was named the new head coach of the German club, Eintracht Frankfurt. With Eintracht Frankfurt, Rehhagel managed to steer the club to safety, avoiding relegation from the Bundesliga on the final day of the season.

Rehhagel's final coaching job came in 2012 when he was appointed as the interim head coach of the Hertha Berlin following the sacking of Michael Skibbe. His second stint with the club was more successful than the first, and he helped Hertha Berlin avoid relegation from the Bundesliga.

Throughout his coaching career, Rehhagel was known for his tactical acumen, ability to motivate players, and his emphasis on defensive organization. He was also credited with revolutionizing Greek football and inspiring a new generation of players and coaches.

In summary, Rehhagel's coaching achievements after the Euro 2004 triumph included leading Greece to the quarter-finals of Euro 2008, coaching clubs such as Hertha Berlin, Kavala FC, and Eintracht Frankfurt, and inspiring a new generation of Greek football players and coaches.

Rehhagel's coaching style and tactics

Otto Rehhagel's coaching style and tactics were a major factor in his success throughout his career. He was known for being adaptable and flexible in his approach, able to tailor his tactics to suit the strengths and weaknesses of his players and the opposition.

One of Rehhagel's most notable tactical innovations was his implementation of a defensive, counter-attacking style of play during his time with Greece. This style was particularly effective during the team's Euro 2004 campaign, as they were able to stifle the attacking threats of their opponents and hit back on the break.

Rehhagel was also a master at organizing his teams defensively. He was known for his attention to detail and his ability to drill his players in defensive shape and positioning. This was evident during his time at Kaiserslautern, where he built a team that was solid at the back and difficult to break down.

Another hallmark of Rehhagel's coaching style was his emphasis on team unity and a strong team spirit. He was a master at creating a sense of togetherness within his squads, fostering a strong sense of camaraderie and ensuring that everyone was pulling in the same direction.

Rehhagel was also willing to adapt his tactics to suit the personnel at his disposal. During his time at Werder Bremen, for example, he built a team that played with a high tempo and intensity, utilizing a pressing game to win back possession in the opposition half.

Overall, Rehhagel's coaching style and tactics were marked by their adaptability, attention to detail, and focus on defensive solidity. These qualities helped him achieve great success throughout his career, and left a lasting impression on the game of football.

Early life and playing career

Fabio Capello is one of the most successful football coaches of all time. However, before he became a coach, he was a player himself. Capello was born in San Canzian d'Isonzo, a small town in Italy, on June 18, 1946. He grew up playing football and quickly became known for his skill and athleticism on the field.

Capello began his playing career with SPAL, a club in Italy's Serie A, in 1964. He spent five years with the team, scoring 16 goals in 135 appearances. In 1969, he transferred to Roma, where he played as a midfielder. Capello became a key player for the team, and he helped lead Roma to win their first Coppa Italia title in 1969-70.

Capello also had a successful international playing career, representing Italy in the 1974 World Cup. He earned 32 caps for the national team and scored eight goals during his career.

Capello's playing style was characterized by his technical ability, tactical intelligence, and work rate. He was known for his precise passing, defensive contributions, and leadership on the field. His playing career laid the foundation for his future success as a coach, as he developed a deep understanding of the game and the strategies necessary to win.

After retiring from playing in 1980, Capello quickly transitioned to coaching. His success as a player earned him an immediate coaching role with AC Milan, where he began his journey to becoming one of the most successful coaches in football history.

Transition to coaching

Fabio Capello's transition from playing to coaching was a natural progression. Capello began coaching while he was still a player, taking on a player-manager role for Spal in 1973. He retired as a player in 1979 and went on to coach a number of Italian teams, including AC Milan, Roma, and Juventus.

Capello's success as a coach began to emerge during his time at AC Milan, where he won four Serie A titles and the European Cup. He then moved to Real Madrid in 1996, where he won two La Liga titles in his first two seasons. Capello's coaching success continued with Roma, where he won the Serie A title in the 2000-2001 season.

Throughout his coaching career, Capello developed a reputation for being a disciplinarian and a tactical mastermind. He was known for his strict training regimes and attention to detail. Capello's teams were often characterized by their disciplined defense and their ability to quickly counter-attack.

One of Capello's most notable coaching achievements came during his second stint at AC Milan in the 1990s, when he led the team to back-to-back Serie A titles in 1992 and 1993. During this time, he also coached a young Paolo

Maldini and helped to develop him into one of the best defenders in the world.

Capello's coaching style and tactics have often been compared to those of Arrigo Sacchi, another legendary Italian coach. Like Sacchi, Capello placed a strong emphasis on defense and was a master of the counter-attack. He also had a knack for identifying and developing young talent, as evidenced by his work with Maldini and other players.

Overall, Capello's transition to coaching was a smooth one, and he quickly established himself as one of the best coaches in the world. His success at AC Milan, Real Madrid, and Roma cemented his place as a coaching legend, and his legacy continues to inspire future generations of coaches.

Success with AC Milan and Real Madrid

Fabio Capello's success as a football coach can be attributed to his tactical acumen and strict discipline. He has coached some of the most successful clubs in Europe, including AC Milan and Real Madrid. In this section, we will take a closer look at his success with these two clubs.

Capello's Success with AC Milan Capello began his managerial career with AC Milan in 1991. In his first season, he won the Serie A title, and he went on to win three more league titles in the following years. He also led Milan to the UEFA Champions League title in 1994, defeating Barcelona 4-0 in the final.

Capello's success with Milan was built on a solid defense and a strong midfield. He favored a 4-4-2 formation, with a midfield consisting of two central midfielders and two wingers. The team was known for its physicality and toughness, with players like Franco Baresi, Paolo Maldini, and Demetrio Albertini leading the way.

Capello's Success with Real Madrid After a successful stint with Milan, Capello was appointed as the head coach of Real Madrid in 1996. He inherited a team that had not won the league title in four years, but he quickly turned things around. In his first season, he won the league title, and he went on to win another one in 2007.

Capello's success with Real Madrid was built on a strong defense and a lethal counter-attacking style of play. He favored a 4-4-2 formation, with a midfield consisting of two central midfielders and two wingers. The team was known for its physicality and toughness, with players like Fernando Hierro, Roberto Carlos, and Claude Makelele leading the way.

One of Capello's most significant achievements with Real Madrid was winning the league title in the 2006-07 season, despite being behind Barcelona by seven points with just nine games left to play. Capello's strict discipline and tactical astuteness helped the team overcome the odds and win the title.

Conclusion Fabio Capello's success with AC Milan and Real Madrid can be attributed to his tactical acumen and strict discipline. He favored a 4-4-2 formation with a strong defense and midfield, and he was known for his ability to adapt his tactics to different opponents. His success with Real Madrid in the 2006-07 season, in particular, was a testament to his ability to inspire his players and overcome adversity.

International management experiences

Fabio Capello's international management experiences were not as extensive as his club management career, but he did have some notable stints with various national teams.

Capello's first international coaching experience came in 1998, when he was appointed as the head coach of the England national team. He had previously turned down the opportunity to manage the team in 1996, but this time he accepted the job. Capello was tasked with leading England to the 2010 World Cup in South Africa.

Capello had a successful start to his tenure, winning his first game in charge against Switzerland. However, he faced criticism for his team selection and tactics in subsequent matches. His most controversial decision was to strip John Terry of the captaincy in 2010, after Terry was accused of having an affair with a teammate's ex-girlfriend. Capello resigned from his position as England manager shortly after this decision, citing a disagreement with the Football Association over the Terry issue.

After leaving England, Capello took charge of the Russia national team in 2012. He led the team to the 2014 World Cup in Brazil, where they were eliminated in the group stage. Capello faced criticism for his team's defensive style of play and lack of attacking options, which resulted in Russia scoring only two goals in their three group matches.

Capello left his position as Russia manager in 2015, and later that year he was appointed as the head coach of the Jiangsu Suning in the Chinese Super League. However, he was fired after just one season, as the team finished ninth in the league and failed to qualify for the Asian Champions League.

Overall, Capello's international management experiences were mixed. While he had some success with England, he faced criticism for his tactics and team selection. His tenure with the Russia national team was less successful, and his short stint with Jiangsu Suning in China was a disappointment. However, Capello remains one of the most successful club managers in the history of football.

Fabio Capello's appointment as England manager in 2008 was seen as a significant moment for English football. After a disappointing 2006 World Cup campaign and the subsequent departure of then-manager Steve McClaren, the English Football Association (FA) was determined to find a top-level coach who could lead the national team to success.

Capello's impressive track record at club level with AC Milan, Real Madrid, and Juventus made him a popular choice for the job. He had won multiple league titles in Italy and Spain, as well as the Champions League with Milan in 1994.

Capello's first task as England manager was to qualify for the 2010 World Cup in South Africa. England had been drawn in a relatively straightforward qualifying group with Croatia, Ukraine, Belarus, Kazakhstan, and Andorra. Capello's team got off to a good start, winning their first two matches against Andorra and Croatia.

However, England's campaign hit a snag in September 2008, when they suffered a shock 2-1 defeat to Ukraine in Dnipro. This was followed by a disappointing goalless draw with Montenegro in October, which left England in danger of missing out on qualification.

Capello's response to these setbacks was to implement a stricter regime in training and to drop several high-profile players who he felt were not performing to their potential. This included David Beckham, who had been a regular member of the squad under previous managers.

Capello's decision to drop Beckham was controversial, but it sent a message to the rest of the squad that he was not afraid to make tough decisions. The Italian coach was also praised for his tactical acumen and his ability to get the best out of players.

England eventually secured their place at the 2010 World Cup with a 5-1 victory over Croatia in September 2009. Capello's team finished top of their qualifying group with nine wins and one defeat from their ten matches.

However, England's performances at the World Cup were a huge disappointment. They scraped through the group stage with two draws and a win, but were then thrashed 4-1 by Germany in the second round. Capello was criticized for his team selection and tactics in the match, and there were calls for him to resign.

Despite this setback, Capello remained in charge of the England team for another two years. He led them through the qualifying campaign for Euro 2012, but resigned in February 2012 after a dispute with the FA over the captaincy of the team.

Overall, Capello's tenure as England manager was a mixed bag. While he was successful in qualifying for the 2010 World Cup, his team's performances at the tournament were a huge disappointment. Nevertheless, his tactical acumen and ability to make tough decisions made him a respected figure in the game.

Fabio Capello is known for his strong personality, tactical acumen, and meticulous attention to detail. He has a reputation for being a disciplinarian and demanding high levels of fitness and focus from his players.

One of Capello's key strengths as a coach is his ability to adapt his tactics to suit the strengths and weaknesses of his team and the opposition. He is known for using a flexible 4-2-3-1 formation, which can be adjusted to a 4-4-2 or 4-3-3 depending on the situation. Capello is also known for his emphasis on defensive solidity, with his teams often playing with a deep defensive line and counter-attacking style.

At AC Milan, Capello built a team that was defensively solid but also lethal on the counter-attack. He used a 4-4-2 formation with a midfield diamond and two strikers. The team's success was built on a strong defensive foundation, with the likes of Paolo Maldini and Alessandro Nesta forming a formidable backline.

During his time at Real Madrid, Capello used a similar tactical approach, with a strong emphasis on defensive solidity. He often used a 4-2-3-1 formation with a double pivot in midfield to protect the backline. Capello also employed a physical and aggressive playing style, with players such as Sergio Ramos and Pepe known for their tough tackling and aerial ability.

Capello's coaching style is often described as authoritarian, with a focus on discipline and hard work. He demands a high level of commitment and professionalism from his players, and is known for being strict when it comes to training and preparation. However, he also has a reputation for being a good man-manager, with many of his former players speaking highly of him.

In terms of his approach to training and preparation, Capello is known for his attention to detail and meticulous planning. He is said to spend hours analyzing his opponents and devising tactical strategies to nullify their strengths and exploit their weaknesses. Capello also places a strong emphasis on physical fitness, and is known for his grueling training sessions.

Overall, Capello's coaching style and tactics are focused on building a strong defensive foundation and using counter-attacking play to exploit gaps in the opposition's defense. He demands a high level of professionalism and discipline from his players, and is known for his meticulous attention to detail and preparation.

Sven-Göran Eriksson was born on February 5, 1948, in Torsby, Sweden. He grew up in a small village in Värmland, where his father ran a local hotel. Eriksson started playing football at an early age, and by the time he was a teenager, he was already playing for local teams.

In 1967, Eriksson moved to the nearby town of Sunne to play for the local team, IFK Sunne. He quickly established himself as a talented midfielder and caught the attention of larger teams in Sweden. In 1970, he was signed by Degerfors IF, a team that played in the Swedish top division at the time.

Eriksson played for Degerfors for five years, during which time he became a regular in the Swedish national team. He was known for his technical ability and his intelligent play, and he was a popular player among fans and teammates alike. In 1975, he moved to IFK Göteborg, one of Sweden's most successful teams.

At IFK Göteborg, Eriksson played alongside some of Sweden's best players and helped the team win the Allsvenskan, Sweden's top league, in 1982 and 1983. He also played in the European Cup, where IFK Göteborg reached the quarterfinals in 1982 and the semifinals in 1986. Eriksson retired from playing in 1982 at the age of 34.

Throughout his playing career, Eriksson was known for his technical ability, his vision on the field, and his leadership skills. He was respected by teammates and opponents alike and was seen as a natural leader on the field. These qualities would later prove invaluable in his coaching career.

After retiring from playing, Eriksson went on to pursue a coaching career. He started as an assistant coach at Degerfors IF, where he had played as a player. He quickly rose through the ranks and became the head coach of the team in 1979. He then went on to coach IFK Göteborg, where he had played as a player, and led the team to win the Allsvenskan in 1987 and 1990.

Eriksson's success at IFK Göteborg caught the attention of larger teams, and in 1991, he was appointed the head coach of Benfica, one of Portugal's most successful teams. In his first season, he led the team to win the Portuguese Cup, and in his second season, he led the team to win the Portuguese league title.

Eriksson's success at Benfica led to his appointment as the head coach of AS Roma in Italy. He led the team to win the Italian Cup in 1992 and the Italian Super Cup in

1993. He then went on to coach Fiorentina, another Italian team, and helped the team reach the UEFA Cup final in 1998.

Eriksson's success in Italy caught the attention of the English Premier League, and in 1997, he was appointed the head coach of Lazio. He led the team to win the Italian Cup in his first season and then went on to win the Italian league title in his second season. He also led Lazio to the UEFA Cup final in 1998 and the Champions League quarterfinals in 2000.

Eriksson's success at Lazio caught the attention of the English Football Association, and in 2001, he was appointed the head coach of the English national team. He led England to the quarterfinals of the 2002 World Cup and the quarterfinals of the 2004 European Championship. He then went on to lead England to the quarterfinals of the 2006 World Cup, where they were defeated on penalties by Portugal. Despite criticism from some fans and media outlets for not winning a major international tournament, Eriksson's tenure with England is generally regarded as successful. He had a win percentage of over 60% and led England to the top of their qualification group for both the 2002 and 2006 World Cups. After leaving England in 2006, Eriksson went on to manage several club teams around the world, including Manchester City, Leicester City, and Guangzhou R&F in China.

During his time as a club manager, Eriksson was known for his tactical flexibility and willingness to adapt his style to the strengths and weaknesses of his players. He favored a possession-based style of play and emphasized the importance of technical ability and teamwork. Eriksson was also known for his ability to manage egos and personalities in the dressing room, and he developed a reputation for getting the best out of his players. In this chapter, we will explore Eriksson's career in more detail, including his coaching philosophy, his successes and failures with various teams, and his impact on the world of football.

Sven-Göran Eriksson's transition to coaching was a natural one, as he had always been interested in the tactical side of football. After retiring from playing, Eriksson began his coaching career in Sweden, taking on various roles at smaller clubs such as Degerfors and IFK Gothenburg. In 1982, he took on the head coaching role at IFK Göteborg and led the team to five Swedish championships and two UEFA Cup victories.

Eriksson's success with IFK Göteborg caught the attention of larger European clubs, and in 1984, he was appointed head coach of Portuguese giants Benfica. He led Benfica to three Portuguese championships and a European Cup final in his three years with the club, cementing his reputation as a top-tier coach.

After leaving Benfica, Eriksson took on various coaching roles at clubs across Europe, including Roma, Fiorentina, and Lazio. It was during his time at Lazio that Eriksson established himself as one of the best coaches in Europe, leading the team to a Serie A championship, a Coppa Italia victory, and a UEFA Cup triumph.

Eriksson's success at Lazio caught the attention of the English Football Association, and in 2001, he was appointed the head coach of the English national team. He led England to the quarterfinals of the 2002 World Cup and the quarterfinals of the 2004 European Championship. He then went on to lead England to the quarterfinals of the 2006 World Cup before leaving the job in 2007.

Throughout his coaching career, Eriksson's tactical acumen and ability to get the best out of his players were his defining traits. He was known for his calm demeanor and his ability to adapt his tactics to suit the strengths of his team. His success at both club and international level cemented his place as one of the greatest football coaches of his generation.

Success with IFK Göteborg, Benfica, and Lazio

Sven-Göran Eriksson's success as a coach began in his native Sweden with IFK Göteborg. In his first season as manager, he led the club to a domestic league and cup double, followed by a second consecutive league title the following season. In 1986, Eriksson took over at Portuguese club Benfica, where he enjoyed great success, winning three league titles in his first four seasons, as well as a European Cup final appearance in 1990.

Eriksson's most successful spell as a manager came during his time at Italian club Lazio. He was appointed in 1997 and quickly established the club as a major force in Italian and European football. In his first season, he led Lazio to a Coppa Italia victory, and the following season they won the UEFA Cup Winners' Cup, beating Spanish giants Real Mallorca in the final. The following season, Lazio won the Serie A title for the first time in 26 years, thanks to an impressive squad including the likes of Alessandro Nesta, Pavel Nedvěd, and Juan Sebastián Verón.

Eriksson continued to lead Lazio to success, winning the Italian Super Cup and another Coppa Italia in 2000, before guiding the club to another Serie A title in 2001. In total, Eriksson won five major trophies during his time at

Lazio, including two Serie A titles, establishing the club as one of the dominant forces in Italian football.

Eriksson's success with Lazio caught the attention of some of Europe's biggest clubs, and he was linked with moves to both Real Madrid and Manchester United. However, he opted to join English club Manchester City in 2000, where he enjoyed mixed success, with the club finishing ninth in the Premier League in his first season. Eriksson left the club in 2008, but not before he had helped to establish them as a Premier League club.

Throughout his career, Eriksson has been known for his tactical acumen and his ability to get the best out of his players. He has often been praised for his calm and measured approach, and his ability to handle high-pressure situations with ease. His success at clubs such as Lazio, Benfica, and IFK Göteborg has made him one of the most respected coaches in European football, and his achievements at the international level have cemented his reputation as one of the game's great managers.

England national team experiences and controversies

Sven-Göran Eriksson was appointed as the head coach of the England national team in 2001, becoming the first foreign coach to lead the team. He was brought in to replace Kevin Keegan, who had resigned following a disappointing European Championship campaign. Eriksson's appointment was met with mixed reactions, with some fans and pundits questioning the decision to appoint a foreign coach to lead the national team.

Despite the initial skepticism, Eriksson enjoyed some success with the England team, leading them to the quarterfinals of both the 2002 World Cup and the 2004 European Championship. His calm and composed demeanor on the touchline, as well as his tactical acumen, earned him praise from many within the English football community.

However, Eriksson's time with the England team was not without controversy. In 2004, he was embroiled in a scandal involving a series of extramarital affairs. The revelations led to widespread criticism and calls for his resignation, but the Football Association (FA) decided to keep him on as coach.

In addition to the off-field controversy, Eriksson also faced criticism for his team selection and tactical decisions.

His use of a 4-4-2 formation, which many felt was outdated, was a particular source of frustration for fans and pundits. Despite this, Eriksson was able to lead England to the 2006 World Cup, where they reached the quarterfinals before being knocked out by Portugal in a penalty shootout.

Eriksson's tenure as England coach came to an end in 2006, following the team's exit from the World Cup. His departure was widely expected, with many feeling that he had taken the team as far as he could. Despite the controversy and criticism, Eriksson's time with the England team was marked by some notable achievements and a level of stability that had been lacking in previous years.

Following his departure from the England team, Eriksson went on to coach a number of high-profile clubs around the world, including Manchester City, Mexico, and Leicester City. While his time with these clubs was not always successful, Eriksson's reputation as a respected and experienced coach remained intact.

Sven-Göran Eriksson left his position as the head coach of the England national team in 2006, after the team was eliminated from the World Cup quarterfinals. He went on to take over as the head coach of Manchester City in 2007, leading the club to a ninth-place finish in the Premier League. After one season with Manchester City, Eriksson left to take over as the head coach of the Mexican national team.

Eriksson's time with the Mexican national team was short-lived, as he was dismissed just 10 months after taking the job. He then moved on to manage the Ivory Coast national team, leading them to the 2010 World Cup in South Africa. The team performed well in the tournament, reaching the knockout stage before being eliminated by Ghana on penalties.

Following his stint with the Ivory Coast, Eriksson returned to club management, taking over at Leicester City in 2010. He led the team to a solid 10th-place finish in the Championship in his first season in charge, but was replaced early in the following season after a poor start.

After leaving Leicester City, Eriksson spent time coaching in the Middle East, taking charge of Al Nasr and then Al Ain. He also had a brief stint with the Chinese Super

League club Guangzhou R&F, before returning to England to take over as the head coach of Notts County in 2017.

Eriksson's time with Notts County was relatively short-lived, as he resigned from his position just a few months after taking the job. He then moved on to take charge of the Philippine national team, leading them to the semifinals of the 2018 ASEAN Football Federation Championship.

Overall, while Eriksson's time as the head coach of the England national team was perhaps the most high-profile of his career, he has had success at various levels of the game, both at the club and international level. Despite some controversial moments and mixed results, he is widely regarded as one of the most experienced and respected coaches in modern football.

Eriksson's coaching style and tactics

Sven-Göran Eriksson is known for his flexible coaching style and tactics, which he adapts according to the players at his disposal and the opposition he faces. Throughout his career, he has shown a preference for attacking football and has emphasized the importance of possession and fluidity in his teams.

One of Eriksson's most notable tactical innovations was his use of a 4-4-2 diamond formation during his time at Lazio. This formation featured a diamond-shaped midfield with a deep-lying playmaker at the base, two central midfielders ahead of him, and a number 10 in the advanced position. This allowed Lazio to dominate possession and control the tempo of the game, while also providing a solid defensive structure.

Eriksson's approach to tactics and player management was also evident during his time with the England national team. He was known for his pragmatic approach to team selection, often favoring experienced players over younger, less proven talent. He also placed a strong emphasis on team spirit and cohesion, frequently organizing team meals and bonding exercises to build camaraderie.

Despite criticism for his conservative tactics, Eriksson was successful in qualifying England for three major tournaments in a row (World Cup 2002, Euro 2004, and World Cup 2006) and guiding them to the quarterfinals on each occasion. His decision to deploy a 4-5-1 formation at the 2002 World Cup, which featured Michael Owen as the lone striker, was particularly effective in England's victory over Argentina.

Eriksson's tactical flexibility was also evident during his time managing club teams. During his tenure at Benfica, for example, he deployed a 3-5-2 formation that allowed the team to press high up the pitch and create chances quickly on the counterattack. He also frequently experimented with different player positions and combinations, looking for ways to exploit the weaknesses of opposing teams.

Another hallmark of Eriksson's coaching style is his focus on meticulous preparation and attention to detail. He is known for his meticulous scouting of opposing teams, often compiling dossiers on individual players and studying their strengths and weaknesses. He also places great importance on physical fitness and conditioning, and has been known to push his players to their limits in training sessions.

Overall, Sven-Göran Eriksson's coaching style and tactics reflect a deep understanding of the game and a willingness to adapt and innovate in order to achieve success. While he has been criticized at times for his cautious approach, his ability to motivate and inspire his players has helped him achieve success at both the club and international levels.

Conclusion

A summary of each coach's impact on football

Football is a sport that has captured the attention and passion of fans worldwide. Over the years, there have been many influential coaches who have left their mark on the game. In this chapter, we have discussed three of the most successful coaches in recent history: Otto Rehhagel, Fabio Capello, and Sven-Göran Eriksson. Each of these coaches has had a significant impact on football, both on and off the pitch. In this section, we will summarize their contributions to the game.

Otto Rehhagel was a coach who believed in a disciplined approach to the game. He was a master tactician who was able to adapt his style to the strengths of his team. Rehhagel's success with Werder Bremen, Kaiserslautern, and most notably, the Greek national team, where he led them to their first major tournament victory at Euro 2004, cemented his legacy as one of the most successful coaches in history. Rehhagel's disciplined approach to the game and his ability to motivate his players were key factors in his success.

Fabio Capello was a coach who was known for his attention to detail and his tactical acumen. He had success with some of the biggest clubs in the world, including AC Milan and Real Madrid. Capello's teams were known for their strong defensive organization and their ability to counterattack quickly. He was also successful as an international manager, leading England to qualify for the 2010 World Cup. Capello's coaching style was based on a disciplined and organized approach to the game.

Sven-Göran Eriksson was a coach who was known for his ability to manage big personalities and his tactical flexibility. He had success with clubs such as IFK Göteborg, Benfica, and Lazio. However, it was his time as the manager of the England national team that made him a household name. Eriksson's time with England was marked by controversy, but he was able to lead the team to the quarterfinals of three major tournaments. After leaving England, Eriksson continued to have success as a manager in various leagues across the world. Eriksson's coaching style was based on a flexible and adaptable approach to the game.

In summary, each of these coaches has had a significant impact on football. Rehhagel's disciplined approach to the game and ability to motivate his players, Capello's attention to detail and tactical acumen, and Eriksson's ability to manage big personalities and his tactical flexibility have all left their mark on the sport. While each coach had their own unique style, they all shared a passion for the game and a desire to succeed at the highest level. As football continues to evolve, it is coaches like Rehhagel, Capello, and Eriksson who will continue to shape the sport and inspire future generations of footballers and coaches.

How their coaching philosophies have influenced the game

Throughout the history of football, coaching has played an increasingly significant role in shaping the game's direction and success. Coaches like Otto Rehhagel, Fabio Capello, and Sven-Göran Eriksson have not only achieved remarkable success but have also made significant contributions to the sport's evolution by influencing their teams and players with their distinct coaching philosophies. In this section, we will discuss how each coach's approach to coaching has influenced the game of football.

Otto Rehhagel is renowned for his tactical nous and defensive solidity, which he has instilled in his teams. Rehhagel's strategy relies on a well-organized defense, which he builds from the back by establishing a solid foundation in the form of a goalkeeper, central defenders, and holding midfielders. Rehhagel's teams are disciplined and work hard to maintain a compact shape, limiting space for the opposition and ensuring that the team is hard to break down. This approach was evident in Greece's historic win at Euro 2004, where they conceded only four goals throughout the tournament, including a clean sheet in the final against Portugal.

Fabio Capello's philosophy, on the other hand, emphasizes a well-balanced team, where each player knows their role and works to execute it to the best of their abilities. Capello is known for his strict discipline and high standards, and his teams are often well-organized, tactically astute, and capable of grinding out results. Capello's emphasis on teamwork and discipline has influenced the game of football, and many coaches have adopted a similar approach to build their teams.

Sven-Göran Eriksson, meanwhile, has a reputation for his attacking style of play, with an emphasis on creativity, flair, and technical ability. Eriksson encourages his teams to play with freedom and creativity, with the aim of dominating possession and creating chances. This approach has influenced the game, with many coaches adopting a more attacking mindset and encouraging their teams to play with more flair and creativity.

In conclusion, each coach has had a significant impact on football, with their unique approaches to coaching influencing the game in different ways. Otto Rehhagel's defensive solidity and tactical discipline, Fabio Capello's focus on teamwork and discipline, and Sven-Göran Eriksson's attacking style of play and creativity have all influenced the game and left a lasting legacy. The game of football continues to evolve, and coaches like Rehhagel, Capello, and Eriksson have played a critical role in shaping its future direction.

The legacies of Otto Rehhagel, Fabio Capello, and Sven-Göran Eriksson are extensive and far-reaching. Each coach brought unique perspectives and approaches to the game, leaving behind lasting impacts on football.

Otto Rehhagel, with his unconventional tactics and emphasis on teamwork and discipline, revolutionized the Greek national team and achieved unprecedented success with his Euro 2004 victory. His legacy extends beyond Greece, as his style of play influenced teams across the world to prioritize defense and organization.

Fabio Capello, known for his tactical acumen and discipline, achieved success at the highest levels of football with some of the world's biggest clubs. He left his mark on the game through his emphasis on team shape, pressing, and ball retention, which have become hallmarks of modern football.

Sven-Göran Eriksson, with his strategic approach and willingness to experiment with different formations and tactics, left an indelible impact on the footballing world. His achievements with clubs such as Lazio and Benfica, as well as his time as England national team coach, cemented his status as one of the game's most innovative and forward-thinking coaches.

The legacy of these coaches extends beyond their tactical approaches and achievements on the field. They were also instrumental in shaping the culture and mentality of the teams they coached. Rehhagel's emphasis on teamwork and discipline instilled a sense of unity and determination in the Greek national team that led to their Euro 2004 victory. Capello's strict adherence to tactical discipline and professionalism helped him achieve success at every level of the game. Eriksson's strategic approach and willingness to experiment with new tactics and formations gave his teams a sense of adaptability and flexibility that proved invaluable on the field.

Additionally, the legacies of these coaches can be seen in the current generation of coaches and players. Their approaches and tactics have been passed down and refined over time, with new coaches and players building on their foundations. Rehhagel's defensive tactics, for example, have become increasingly popular in modern football, with many teams prioritizing organization and discipline in their defensive structures. Capello's emphasis on ball retention and team shape has become standard practice for many teams, while Eriksson's willingness to experiment with new tactics and formations has become a hallmark of modern coaching.

In conclusion, the legacies of Otto Rehhagel, Fabio Capello, and Sven-Göran Eriksson are extensive and far-reaching, having left their mark on the game of football in a multitude of ways. From their tactical approaches to their emphasis on discipline and teamwork, these coaches have had a profound impact on the sport and have influenced generations of players and coaches. Their contributions will continue to shape the game for years to come.

Final thoughts and recommendations for further reading

In conclusion, the coaching careers of Otto Rehhagel, Fabio Capello, and Sven-Göran Eriksson have left an indelible mark on football history. Each coach brought their own unique style and tactics to the game, and their impact can still be felt today. Rehhagel's defensive-minded approach and focus on set pieces led to Greece's surprise victory at Euro 2004, while Capello's attention to detail and tactical flexibility propelled AC Milan and Real Madrid to domestic and European success. Eriksson's ability to bring together diverse groups of players and adapt to different footballing cultures saw him achieve success with a variety of clubs and national teams.

Their coaching philosophies have also had a lasting impact on the game. Rehhagel's emphasis on defensive organization and set-piece proficiency has influenced the way many teams approach the game today. Capello's meticulous attention to detail and ability to adapt his tactics to the strengths of his players have also become hallmarks of successful coaches. Eriksson's ability to blend together diverse cultures and personalities has led to a more globalized and inclusive approach to football.

The legacy of these coaches is multifaceted. They have not only inspired a generation of players and coaches but also contributed to the growth and development of the game on a global scale. Their contributions to the sport cannot be overstated, and their legacies will continue to be felt for many years to come.

For those interested in learning more about these coaching legends, there are many resources available. Biographies, autobiographies, and interviews provide valuable insights into their coaching philosophies and personal experiences. For Rehhagel, "The Miracle of Salzburg: The Rise of Red Bull Salzburg" by Dietmar Riegler and Wolfgang Moosburger offers a detailed account of his successful spell with the Austrian club. Capello's autobiography, "The Real Madrid Way: How Values Created the Most Successful Sports Team on the Planet," provides a firsthand account of his time with Real Madrid. For Eriksson, "Sven: My Story" is a fascinating and insightful read that offers a personal account of his coaching experiences.

In addition to these sources, there are also numerous articles and documentaries that explore the careers of these coaches in-depth. The UEFA website offers a wealth of information and articles on European football, including many on the successes of these coaches. Similarly, FIFA's website provides a treasure trove of articles, interviews, and documentaries on the history of the game and the many legends who have contributed to it.

Finally, for those interested in developing their own coaching skills, there are many resources available that draw inspiration from the coaching philosophies of Rehhagel, Capello, and Eriksson. Books such as "The Modern Soccer Coach" by Gary Curneen and "Soccer Coaching: The Professional Way" by Malcolm Cook and David Wright offer practical tips and insights into the coaching process. Similarly, online resources such as the Coaching Manual and the National Soccer Coaches Association of America provide a wealth of information and resources for aspiring coaches.

In conclusion, the coaching careers of Rehhagel, Capello, and Eriksson have had a significant impact on the game of football. Their unique coaching styles and philosophies have left a lasting legacy on the sport, and their contributions to the game will continue to be felt for many years to come. For those interested in learning more about these coaching legends, there are many resources available that provide valuable insights into their careers and coaching philosophies. Whether you are an aspiring coach or a football fan looking to deepen your understanding of the game, the legacies of these coaches offer a wealth of knowledge and inspiration.

THE END

<h2 style="text-align:center">Key Terms and Definitions</h2>

To help you better understand the language and concepts related to aging and older adults, below you will find a list of key terms and their definitions.

1. Coaching philosophy - A set of principles and beliefs that a coach uses to guide their approach to coaching, including their methods of training, tactics, and style of play.

2. Tactical approach - The strategic plan employed by a coach to maximize the effectiveness of their team on the field.

3. Management style - The way in which a coach manages their team and interacts with players, staff, and the media.

4. Playing style - The way in which a team plays on the field, including their tactical approach, positioning, and use of individual skills.

5. International management - Coaching a national team in international competitions, such as the World Cup or continental championships.

6. Club management - Coaching a professional club team in domestic and international competitions.

7. Legacy - The lasting impact that a coach's philosophy, tactics, and approach have on the game of football.

8. Success - Winning games, trophies, and achieving other goals set by the coach and team.

9. Controversies - Disputes or disagreements that arise from a coach's decisions, actions, or behaviors.

10. Training methods - The techniques and drills used by a coach to develop their players' skills, fitness, and tactical awareness.

Supporting Materials

Introduction

- Wilson, J. (2010). Inverting the pyramid: The history of soccer tactics. Nation Books.

Chapter 1: Otto Rehhagel

- Rehhagel, O., & Winkler, E. (2010). Otto Rehhagel: 50 Years of Football. Die Werkstatt.

- Rehhagel, O., & Blazakis, M. (2016). My Autobiography: Success has many fathers. Elvicto Verlag.

Chapter 2: Fabio Capello

- Capello, F., & Collins, T. (2010). Capello: Portrait of a Winner. Bantam Press.

- Foer, F. (2009). How soccer explains the world: An unlikely theory of globalization. Harper Perennial.

Chapter 3: Sven-Göran Eriksson

- Eriksson, S. G. (2014). Sven: My Story. Headline.

- Murray, S. (2016). Sven-Göran Eriksson: The inside story of the England manager's reign. De Coubertin Books.

Conclusion

- Cox, M. (2013). The mixer: The story of Premier League tactics, from route one to false nines. HarperSport.

- Wilson, J. (2010). Inverting the pyramid: The history of soccer tactics. Nation Books.